Life Cycles

D0493720

By the end of this book you will know more about:

- How plants reproduce.

- Pollination and germination.

- Animals and their life cycles.

You will:

- Use Fact Files, books, the Internet and CD-ROMs to help you answer questions.

- Carry out a scientific enquiry.

- Record results in a table.

- Create bar charts and graphs.

Flowering plants reproduce.

Task 1

What are your ideas about seeds and fruit?

1

These children are discussing a flowering plant.

 Do you agree with what they say?

★ Use part of Task Sheet 1 to show your ideas about where you think seeds come from.

> **The plant makes seeds. Parts of the flower make the seed.**

> **Seeds come from shops and garden centres. A factory makes the seeds.**

> **A special leaf changes into a fruit or a pod. You find the seeds inside the fruit or the pod.**

Task 2

Where do seeds come from?

★ Look at these pictures. Each line starts with a seed and goes backwards to show where it came from. What does the last picture in each line show?

★ Now draw pictures of three more seeds and the flowers they came from. Use CD-ROMs, the Internet and reference books to help you.

Orange tree

The seed   *...and before that*   *...and before that*   *...and before that.*

Dandelion

2 *The seed*   *...and before that*   *...and before that*   *...and before that.*

Fact File

Finding fruits

A fruit is the part of a plant that carries the seeds.

Fruits come in all shapes and sizes. Here are some of them.

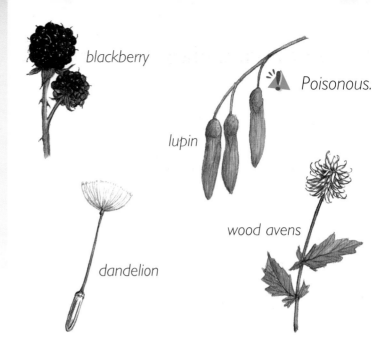

blackberry

Poisonous.

lupin

wood avens

dandelion

Go on a fruit hunt

fruit

seed

✦ Look for fruits on all types of flowering plants. Remember, a fruit is the part of the plant that carries the seeds. Sometimes you can spot fruits beginning to grow before the flower dies.

✦ Choose one fruit. Carefully draw the outside.

✦ Ask an adult to cut it in half. Find the seeds inside.

✦ Use a magnifier. Draw a seed.

✦ Now look at more fruits, such as oranges and lemons.

- Why are the two ends of the fruit different?

- Which parts do we eat?

- Where are the seeds?

- Why do plants need so many seeds?

✦ Draw the cut fruit and label it.

⚠ *Ask an adult to cut the fruit when you are ready to draw the inside. Check with an adult before you touch any plant.*

Baked beans

Humans and other animals eat fruits and seeds produced by plants. One of the most popular British foods is baked beans. The beans in a tin of baked beans are the seeds of a bean plant.

 ## Seed dispersal

Once the seed is fully formed it is ready to make a new plant. Plants make lots of seeds but most seeds will not grow into new plants. They get eaten, destroyed or damaged or end up somewhere where plants can't grow.

The seed has a better chance of surviving if it does not land right next to the parent plant. This is because the parent plant may take the light and water that the new plant needs to grow.

When seeds travel away from their parent plant we call it **seed dispersal**. Seeds can be dispersed by wind, explosion, water, and animals.

lupin

Poisonous.

wood avens

ash

blackberry

coconut

dandelion

Seeds are dispersed in different ways.

Talking seeds

I've got a juicy covering. Birds find it really tasty. They eat up the fruit. I go right through the bird and come out the other end. I can travel miles this way.

Copy these speech bubbles. Read the Fact File on seed dispersal and write the correct name of the plant next to each speech bubble.

- dandelion
- blackberry
- wood avens
- lupin
- ash
- coconut

I'm light as a feather. The wind catches me and blows me away. I've got my own tiny parachute. It helps to keep me in the air.

Use Task Sheet 2 to show how different plants disperse their seeds.

I sit in a pod with lots of other seeds. When the pod is ripe it splits open suddenly and twists at the same time. All the seeds explode out of the pod.

I hitch a ride on any passing animal. I've got hooks that stick out to catch in their fur.

I am large and hollow with a thick coat. When I fall off a tree and drop in the sea I float. The sea may carry me for hundreds of kilometres before I wash up on a shore.

I've got a wing attached to me. It makes a brilliant spinner. When the wind catches it, I go spinning away.

Plants reproduce.

Poppy population

There are four types of red poppy growing in the British Isles.
The poppy fruit is a capsule containing thousands of tiny black seeds. Look at the photograph of the capsules. Each capsule looks as if it has a hat. Just under the hat you should be able to see small holes. It looks a bit like a pepperpot. The seeds are shaken out of the holes when the capsule sways in the wind. The seeds are dispersed by the wind.

Poppy

Capsules containing poppy seeds

The maps show you two things: where each type of poppy grows and approximately how many poppies grow there. More dots mean more poppies.

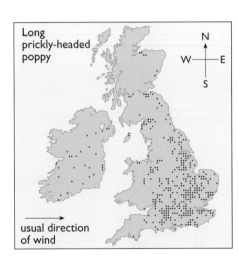

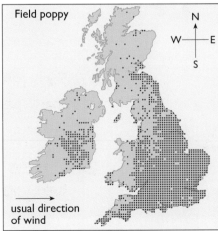

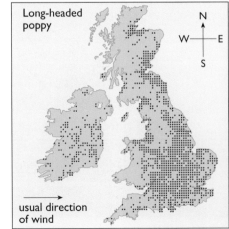

✵ Look at this table.

Name of poppy	Number of seeds made by one plant
Field poppy	about 170 000
Long-headed poppy	about 14 000
Long prickly-headed poppy	about 2 000
Rough poppy	about 1 500

✵ Use the information from the maps and the table to answer these questions.

1 Which is the commonest poppy? How do you know?

2 Which is the rarest? How do you know?

3 Do more poppies grow in the west or the east of Britain?

4 Poppy seeds are dispersed by the wind. What do you think the maps might look like if poppies were dispersed by animals and not by the wind?

Words to learn and use:
capsule
fruit
flower
seed
seed dispersal

Extra Challenge

✵ Each year on Remembrance Day, many people wear poppies. Find out why this is?

✵ Use the Internet and CD-ROMs to help you find the answer.

⭐ **Seeds need the right conditions to germinate.**
Plan and carry out a fair test.

Fact File Germination

Most plants make lots of seeds. When the seeds are dispersed, most of them end up in places where they cannot grow. Only a few seeds land in the right place for them to begin to grow or **germinate**.

When a seed starts to germinate a small root called a **radicle** comes out of the seed.

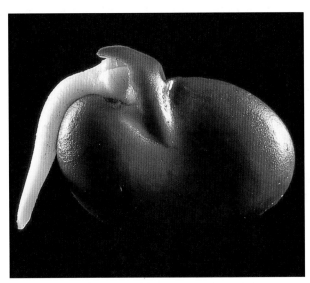

Bean seed with radicle

Task 6

Scientific Enquiry
What do seeds need to germinate?

Class 5 wanted to find out what cress seeds need to germinate. They brainstormed and came up with these ideas.

> We could try germinating cress seeds on wet kitchen paper – some in a warm place and some in the fridge.

> We could try putting some cress seeds on wet kitchen paper and some on dry kitchen paper.

> We could try germinating the seeds in a dark cupboard and in the light.

> We could try germinating the seeds in soil and compost.

✵ In your group discuss with your teacher an idea that you want to test to find out what seeds need to germinate.

✵ Think about:

- How many seeds you will use – lots or just a small spoonful?

- How much water you will use and how you will measure it.

- Where you will keep the germinating seeds and when you will check them.

- When you will know that they have germinated.

✵ Use Task Sheet 3 to plan your investigation. Carry it out and then answer these questions:

1 How do your findings relate to the time of year when most seeds germinate in Britain?

2 Why is spring the time when most seeds germinate?

3 Would autumn be a good time for seeds to germinate? Why?

you need:

- seeds, e.g. cress, radish, spring onion, lettuce, beans, peas

- kitchen paper

- compost and soil

- seed trays or other suitable containers

- labels

- water

- measuring cylinder or beaker

Fact File   Desert seeds

In some hot deserts of the world, the soil contains many seeds waiting to germinate. Special coats stop the seeds germinating until enough rain has fallen to wash them away. After a good drenching the seeds germinate, quickly flower and produce more seeds before the drought returns. When rain reaches these deserts, the ground may be covered in a colourful carpet of flowers for just a short time. The desert plants take advantage of the precious water to continue their life cycle.

⭐ Plants produce flowers, fruits and seeds.

A closer look at a flower

Flowers are essential to the life cycle of flowering plants.
A flower is made up of several different parts.

✿ Look at the picture below. It shows you what you might see if you cut a flower in half.

This is a cherry tree. It has pink flowers.

Each flower looks like this.

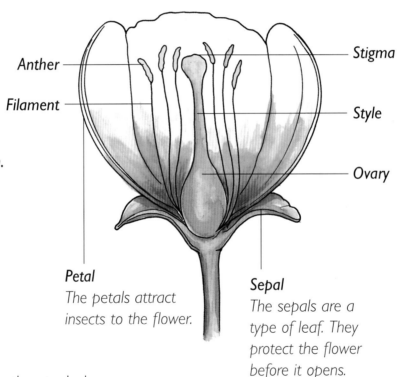

*Together these parts make the male part of the flower. This is called the **stamen**. The stamen makes the pollen.*

Anther

Filament

Stigma

Style

Ovary

*Together these parts make the female part of the flower. This is called the **carpel** or **pistil**. The female parts make the seeds.*

Petal
The petals attract insects to the flower.

Sepal
The sepals are a type of leaf. They protect the flower before it opens.

✿ Use this information to help you complete this table.

Part of flower	Special features	Job/purpose
	Green leaves.	Protects flower before it opens.
Stamen		
		Female part of flower that makes seeds.
	Often coloured and scented.	

Taking flowers apart

4

If you take a flower apart very carefully you can see all the different parts.
You can stick them on to card to make a flower card.
These pictures show you how to do it.

Look at the flower card below.
Find the following things on the card.

petal	style	sepal
filament	stamen	stigma
anther	ovary	carpel or pistil

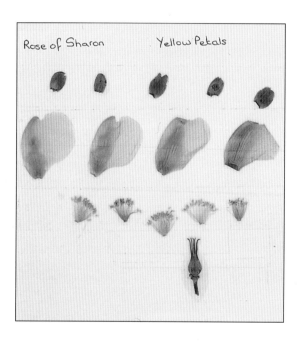

Now complete Task Sheet 4.

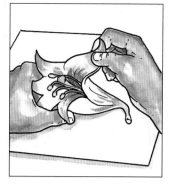

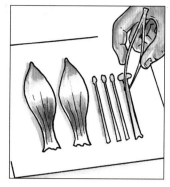

I Put the flower on white paper. Carefully take it apart.

2 You may need to use tweezers to move some of the smaller parts.

3 Stick the parts on to a strip of card. Put the glue on the card, not the flower parts.

4 Let the glue dry. Cover the card with sticky-backed plastic or sticky tape.

Let your teacher know if you are allergic to pollen.

Task
9

Flower identification cards

5

Look at your flower from Task 8. How could you tell it apart from all the others?

Take measurements and draw pictures of your flower to make a flower ID card.

Complete Task Sheet 5.

Flowers need pollinating to make fruits and seeds.

Pollination

All flowering plants make pollen. Each type of plant makes pollen that has special features.

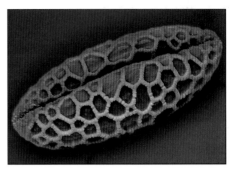

■ Look at these magnified pictures of pollen grains.

● How are they alike? How are they different?

● Which might be best carried by wind? Why?

● Which might be best carried by insects? Why?

■ If possible, collect some pollen and observe it with a magnifying glass or microscope.

Let your teacher know if you are allergic to pollen.

Making the seed

A flowering plant needs to make seeds that are able to grow into new plants. To do this, pollen, from the male part of the plant, must reach the stigma.

When pollen lands on the stigma, we say the plant has been **pollinated**. A lot of plants cannot be pollinated by their own pollen. The pollen must land on another plant of the same type. For example, the pollen from the flower of one cherry tree must reach the stigma of a flower on another cherry tree. This is called **cross-pollination**.

How does pollen travel from one plant to another? Sometimes the wind blows it. Sometimes insects carry the pollen.

Plants that need to attract insects make sugary nectar, which many insects eat. These plants often have beautifully coloured petals and sweet scents to attract insects.

Pollen looks like a fine powder. It is usually a yellowish colour. It is produced in the anther

The stigma is usually slightly sticky on top to help it catch the pollen

Insect pollination

- ✦ In groups, observe some flowering plants in the school garden or nearby habitat.

- How many insects can you see visiting the flowers?

- Which flowers do they visit?

- Are some coloured flowers visited by more insects than others? Why?

- What are the insects collecting from the flowers?

- What are they taking to other flowers?

- ✦ Use your information to write a poem or a story explaining to other children what you have seen.

Insect pollination

Hay fever

In spring and summer, grasses and other flowering plants make millions of pollen grains. Some people are allergic to this pollen and it makes their eyes run and itch. They may also sneeze a lot to get the pollen out of their bodies. This reaction is known as hay fever.

Insects pollinate some flowers.

Task 12   Pollination Street

6

Insects carry the pollen on some plants from one flower to another. Pollen fertilises the female ovule. (The ovule is sometimes called the ovum.)

Here is the start of a strip cartoon. The pollen from one tree has to reach its target – the sticky stigma on the next tree on the other side of the Street.

How can it do this? Complete the cartoon on Task Sheet 6.

Fact File   Getting fertilised

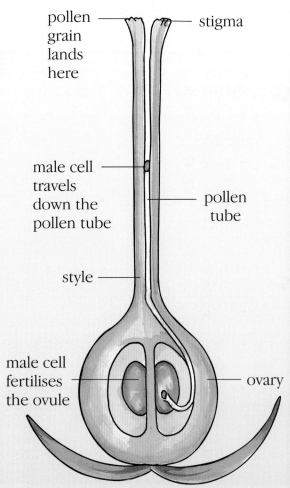

pollen grain lands here — stigma

male cell travels down the pollen tube

pollen tube

style

male cell fertilises the ovule — ovary

When the pollen lands on the sticky stigma, a tiny tube, called a pollen tube, grows down the style and into the middle of the ovary. A special part of the pollen called the male cell goes down the tube and enters the middle of the ovary.

When the male pollen cell reaches the ovary and joins with the female **ovule** we say the plant has been **fertilised**.

After this, seeds start to grow. It is usually the ovary of the flower which becomes the **fruit** containing seeds. In science, a fruit is the part of a plant where seeds develop. It doesn't have to taste good!

Fast plants

 Like all plants, flowering plants have a life cycle.

1 Plants grow flowers.

2 The flowers are pollinated.

3 The fruit grows, then seeds grow in the fruit.

4 The seeds are dispersed.

5 Some of the seeds germinate.

6 They grow into plants.

7 The plants grow flowers, and so the cycle starts again.

Most plants take quite a long time to go through their life cycle. Often it takes a whole year. Special **fast plants** take only about six weeks to go through their life cycle. The table shows information about how fast plants grow.

Use the information in the table to plot a line graph of the plant's height over the first 35 days. Plot your graph on Task Sheet 7. Give it a title.

Use your graph to help you answer these questions.

Life cycle of a fast plant

| 2 days | 4 days | 11 days | 18 days | 28 days |

Time in days	Height above ground in cm
2	1
4	3
7	4
11	8
15	15
18	18
25	20
30	20
35	20

1 When was the plant 8 cm high?

2 What height would you expect the plant to be on day 14?

3 Between which two readings did the plant grow fastest?

4 At the end, the line on your graph is flat. Why is this?

5 What might the plant look like on day 15? Draw a picture.

Animals have a life cycle of birth, growth, reproduction and death.

A

Spot the life cycle

 Look at the photographs.
They show the different stages of the life cycle.
Which photographs show the following:

- birth
- growth
- reproduction
- death?

B

C

D

Now look at the pictures on Task Sheet 8.
Cut out the pictures. Put them in the correct order.

Extra Challenge

Make a glossary, for other children to use. Include these words:

- germinate
- pollinate
- reproduction
- life cycle.

Growing up

 Babies have special needs.
Look at a photograph of you as a baby.

 What did you need when you were a baby?
Draw and write to show your ideas.

 Write a story explaining what you think
happens to your height and weight as
you grow up into adulthood.
Will you stop growing?

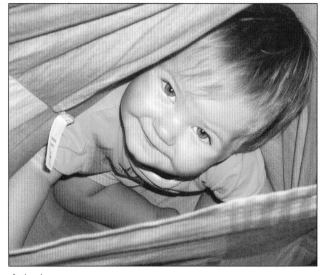

A baby

Keeping the life cycle going

 Look at the
picture. It
shows how
the life cycle
keeps going.

babyhood → childhood → adolescence → adulthood

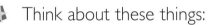

 Draw and write to
show what the different
stages of your life might be
like. You could use a computer
to help you.

parents

 Think about these things:

- What will you look like when you
  are older?

- When might you have children?

- What important things will you have to
  do as a parent?

- What might you be like when you have
  grown old?

- Who might be able to help you when
  you are old?

babyhood → childhood → adolescence → adulthood

parents

baby

 How long do humans depend on parents
or a caring adult?

If living things don't reproduce they die out.

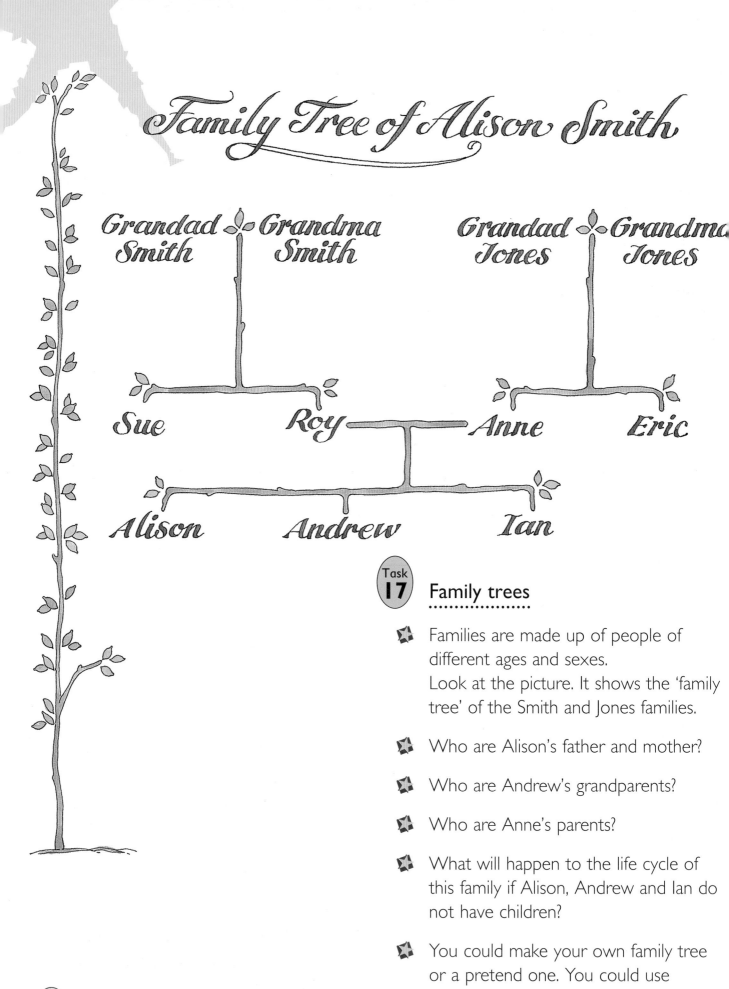

Family Tree of Alison Smith

Grandad Smith — Grandma Smith

Grandad Jones — Grandma Jones

Sue   Roy — Anne   Eric

Alison   Andrew   Ian

Task 17   **Family trees**

- Families are made up of people of different ages and sexes.
  Look at the picture. It shows the 'family tree' of the Smith and Jones families.

- Who are Alison's father and mother?

- Who are Andrew's grandparents?

- Who are Anne's parents?

- What will happen to the life cycle of this family if Alison, Andrew and Ian do not have children?

- You could make your own family tree or a pretend one. You could use drawing and word processing packages.

Fact File Mammal fertilisation

To make a new animal two special cells have to join together. One cell is from the female and is called the **egg**. The other is from the male and is called a **sperm**. When animals **mate** the sperm joins with the egg to fertilise it. Then the egg can start to develop into a new animal. Like most furry animals, humans are mammals. A fertilised mammal egg develops into a baby inside its mother. The time it takes for a mammal to grow and develop before it is born is called the pregnancy or **gestation time**. This time is different for different mammals.

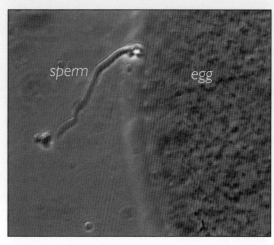

Sperm fertilising the egg

Extra Challenge

✪ Look at the table showing the gestation times for some different mammals.

Animal	Gestation in days	Gestation in weeks
Mouse	21	
Rabbit	30	
Lion	108	
Human	252	
Cow	284	
Horse	336	
Elephant	624	

✪ Copy and complete the table and answer these questions:

1 Which of these mammals has the shortest gestation time?

2 Which of these mammals has the longest gestation time?

3 How long is the gestation time of a human?

4 How many mammals in the table have gestation times longer than that of humans? Which are they?

5 How much longer is an elephant's gestation time than a human's?

6 How does the length of the gestation time appear to be connected to the size of the mammal?

Fact File

Fascinating life cycles

Some animals have special ways of reproducing.

Some female spiders eat the male after mating.

The male three-spined stickleback builds a nest in which the female lays her eggs. The male fertilises the eggs with sperm, then he guards the nest until the young fish hatch. During this time, the male stickleback has a red chest. This is a warning sign to other fish to keep away.

The seahorse is a fish. The female seahorse lays eggs in a pouch on the male seahorse's tummy. When they hatch, tiny seahorse babies come out of the pouch.

Female bats usually have one baby each year. They rarely have twins because the extra weight would make flying difficult for a pregnant bat.

Kangaroos give birth to very tiny babies. After they are born, they climb into a pouch on the mother's tummy to grow. They suck milk made by the mother.

Emperor penguins live in Antarctica. The female lays a single egg. The male holds the egg on his feet under a fold of skin. This keeps the egg warm.

Words to learn and use:
egg
gestation
life cycle
sperm

Life spans

A life span is the time between starting life at birth and ending it with death. Different animals have different life spans. The table gives information about the life spans of some animals, including the longest human life span.

Animals	Life span (years)
chimpanzee	44
Chinese alligator	52
dog	20
eagle owl	68
Galapagos tortoise	100+
herring gull	41
horse	46
house mouse	3
human	120+
Indian elephant	70
monkey	29
vampire bat	13

✿ Make another table of this information using the same headings. Put the animal with the longest life span at the top and the one with the shortest life span at the bottom. You could use a computer spreadsheet.

✿ Make a bar chart of the information in your table.

✿ Use your bar chart to answer these questions:

1 Which animal has the longest life span?

2 Which animal has the shortest life span?

3 How much longer is a vampire bat likely to live than a house mouse?

4 How much longer is an eagle owl likely to live than a herring gull?

5 Why do you think some animals have longer life spans than others?

House mouse

Galapagos tortoise

Task 19 Survival Game

1 Use the board on Task Sheet 9 to play the Survival Game.

2 Each player needs a container (the boat) and six counters in two colours. The counters are the people in your boat – three males and three females. Use different colours for the males and females.

3 Start at the bottom of the board and travel along the squares.

4 Throw a dice to see who starts.

5 Move along the board according to the score on the dice. The squares you land on show how many children are born or how many people die.

6 The winner is the boat that reaches the end with the most males and females in it. If you have all males or all females in the boat, you cannot win. In this game, you have to have a male and female to make more children to keep the life cycle going.

Checkpoint

Endangered species

Some animals and plants are in danger of **extinction**.

Choose and research a rare plant or animal. Use reference books, CD-ROMs and the Internet to help you. Find out how it can be protected so that it survives to reproduce and increase in population.

You could consider:

- a breeding programme
- how to protect it from humans and from other animals
- how to make sure it has enough food
- how the law might be changed.

Make a poster or an illustrated report of your ideas.

Black rhino

Summary

Which of these do you know and which can you do?

- I know that flowering plants reproduce.
- I know that seeds provide food for humans and other animals.
- I know that seeds are dispersed in different ways.
- I know that plants reproduce.
- I know that seeds need the right conditions to germinate.
- I can plan and carry out a fair test.
- I know that plants produce flowers, fruits and seeds.
- I know that flowers need pollinating to make fruits and seeds.
- I know that insects pollinate some flowers.
- I know that animals have a life cycle of birth, growth, reproduction and death.
- I know that if living things don't reproduce they die out.

Complete your **Science Log** to show how well you know these and how well you can do them. Circle a face for each statement.

Glossary

pistil

anther – the part of the stamen that makes pollen.

extinction – when a plant or animal dies out altogether. No more of these plants or animals can ever exist again.

fertilisation – the process of making an egg fertile.

filament – the part of the stamen that carries the anther at its tip.

fruit – the part of a plant that carries seeds.

germination – when seeds sprout and begin to grow.

gestation – the time taken for a mammal to grow inside its mother.

life cycle – the processes that occur throughout the life of a plant or animal.

ovary – the female reproductive organ.

ovule / ovum – an egg cell.

pistil – the female part of a flower consisting of ovary, stigma and style.

pollen – the male reproductive cell of a flower.

reproduce – to produce young.

seed – the bits made by a flower that contain a baby plant ready to grow.

seed dispersal – the spreading of seeds to a new area.

sepal – green leaves that protect a flower before it opens.

stamen – the male part of a flower consisting of the anther and the filament.

stigma – the sticky bit on top of the style.

style – the part of a flower that carries the stigma at its tip.

stamen

seed dispersal